# 从零打造葡萄酒胜地(中国宁夏)

张文晓 / 丽兹·塔什(Liz Thach)
宁夏葡萄与花卉产业发展局 / 美国加利福尼亚索诺玛州立大学

**授权翻译：**
邱继达 / 战先勇

# 从零打造葡萄酒胜地(中国宁夏)

张文晓 / 丽兹·塔什(Liz Thach)
宁夏葡萄与花卉产业发展局 / 美国加利福尼亚索诺玛州立大学

**授权翻译:**

邱继达 / 战先勇

**ISBN-13: 978-1541379381**
**ISBN-10: 1541379381**

—— 节选自《全球葡萄酒旅游的 12 种最佳实践》第四章,Chapter Excerpt from Best Practices in Global Wine Tourism (2016).

https://www.cognizantcommunication.com/

人生得意须尽欢，莫使金樽空对月。
--李白

*When you are in good times, enjoy yourself to the full, the golden cup should be filled with wine accompanied by the moonlight.*
*-- Li Bai*

# 从零打造葡萄酒胜地（中国宁夏）

张文晓 / 丽兹·塔什（Liz Thach）
宁夏葡萄与花卉产业发展局 / 美国加利福尼亚索诺玛州立大学

**授权翻译：**
邱继达 / 战先勇

贺兰山脉顶峰海拔高达 3500 多米，山下的灌溉平原有着 39000 多公顷葡萄园，这正是位于华中地区的宁夏葡萄酒产区。当地葡萄与花卉产业发展局局长曹凯龙先生望了一下远方，山峰上的一尘白雪在这个晴朗的腊月早晨清晰可见。

他面前的沙质平原受到上天恩宠，贺兰山脉的冲击土壤遍布于此，六台大型推土机正在缓缓移动，为宁夏葡萄酒产区开拓着更多的葡萄园。曹局长笑了，他意识到打造一个世界级的葡萄酒旅游胜地的梦想正在逐步实现。他还记得，20 年前的这里仍是一片荒芜，而如今，这个和纳帕谷同处北纬 38 度线的谷地，却出产着不少顶尖的中国葡萄酒，其中包括曾获英国《醇鉴》杂志 2011 年世界葡萄酒大奖的"加贝兰"葡萄酒。

曹局长转向站在他身后的一群正在拍照和做笔记的国际记者，开始讲话。伴随着在严寒空气中清晰可见的呼吸声，他用中文描述了他们在过去几年所取得的进步，口译员干练精准地将其讲话内容译为英法双语，随后进入提问环节。曹局长面带微笑，开心地讲述起这段征途，他和他的团队要从零开始在中国西北地区缔造出一个葡萄酒胜地。

## 中国葡萄酒行业概览

科学家们在河南省出土的古陶器中发现了一些有机残留物，而这些残留物来自由大米，蜂蜜和水果发酵而成的饮料，这证明中国从公元前1600年就开始酿酒了。（"中国文化"，2003年版）。然而在中文里，"Wine"一词被翻译为"酒"，代指任何类型的酒精饮料。所以很有必要使用"葡萄酒"一词来称呼用葡萄酿制的酒。尽管中国拥有自己的本土葡萄品种山葡萄，但几个世纪以来，米酒却远比葡萄酒更受追捧。

18世纪90年代，山东省烟台市诞生了首款使用酿酒葡萄生产的中国葡萄酒。遍游海外的清末外交官、近代著名商人张弼士先生决定在此开设第一家大型酿酒厂，称之为张裕先锋葡萄酒公司（Lyons，2013年）。一开始他从欧洲引入酿酒葡萄插枝，却出现了水土不服难以存活的状况，所以他将这些插枝嫁接到中国本地砧木上，大获成功。最终，他的葡萄酒开始在各类国际比赛中斩获奖牌。今天，张裕是中国最大的酿酒厂之一，在国内各地区坐拥八个大型城堡式酒庄，并拥有多处海外资产（Changyu.com，2014）。

在十九世纪中后期，其他葡萄酒厂终于开始在中国出现，其中包括实力雄厚，生产著名长城牌葡萄酒的国营中粮集团酒庄。根据2014年国际葡萄与葡萄酒组织的统计数据（StatOIV, 2014），中国的葡萄园面积从2000年的30万公顷增长到2011年的56万公顷，在2012年全球葡萄酒产量榜排名第五（OIV，2014）。最新报告也显示，中国目前有625家酒庄(Gastin，2014)。

## 中国主要酿酒葡萄品种

北京中国农业大学教授卢江表示（2015），中国境内种植的葡萄中，有80%是鲜食葡萄，15%是酿酒葡萄，剩下的5%用来制作葡萄干。他指出，中国种植的主要葡萄品种包括赤霞珠(49.6%)，佳美娜(亦称蛇龙珠, 9.6%)，梅洛(8.5%)以及西拉和霞多丽(两者均低于2%)。国内的红葡萄酒销量大于白葡萄酒，主要因为红色代表着喜庆，但也有消息称白葡萄酒在中国的热度正在日渐上升（Lawrence，2012）。

## 中国八大葡萄酒产区

目前中国有八大葡萄酒产区（Johnson & Robinson, 2013）：

**1. 山东产区** - 酿酒历史最悠久，酒庄数量最多的产区，地处突出于黄海的山东半岛，气候更加温和，但高湿度的环境也时常会使葡萄遭受霉菌侵扰；

**2. 新疆产区** - 中国第二大葡萄产区，除酿酒葡萄酒外，还种植很大比例的鲜食葡萄。位于遥远的中国西部，气候干燥，土地贫瘠。在严寒的冬季，需要将葡萄藤埋在地下以起到防护作用。作为中国主要穆斯林聚居地，它还是"古丝绸之路"的一部分，境内有许多城镇从公元前300年就开始了葡萄酒酿造，吐鲁番便是其中之一；（Thach，2009）

**3. 宁夏产区** - 位于中国中部，靠近贺兰山脉，气候干燥，阳光充足，以生产高品质葡萄酒而闻名。虽然冬天也会用掩埋的方式来保护葡萄藤，但这里气候更利于出产健康的葡萄，冲积土壤和流经附近的黄河都为葡萄生长提供了积极条件；

**4. 河北产区** - 位于北京主城区外沿，一些非常大的酿酒厂所在地。凭借着临近长城和颐和园的优势，吸引着大量的游客前来观光；

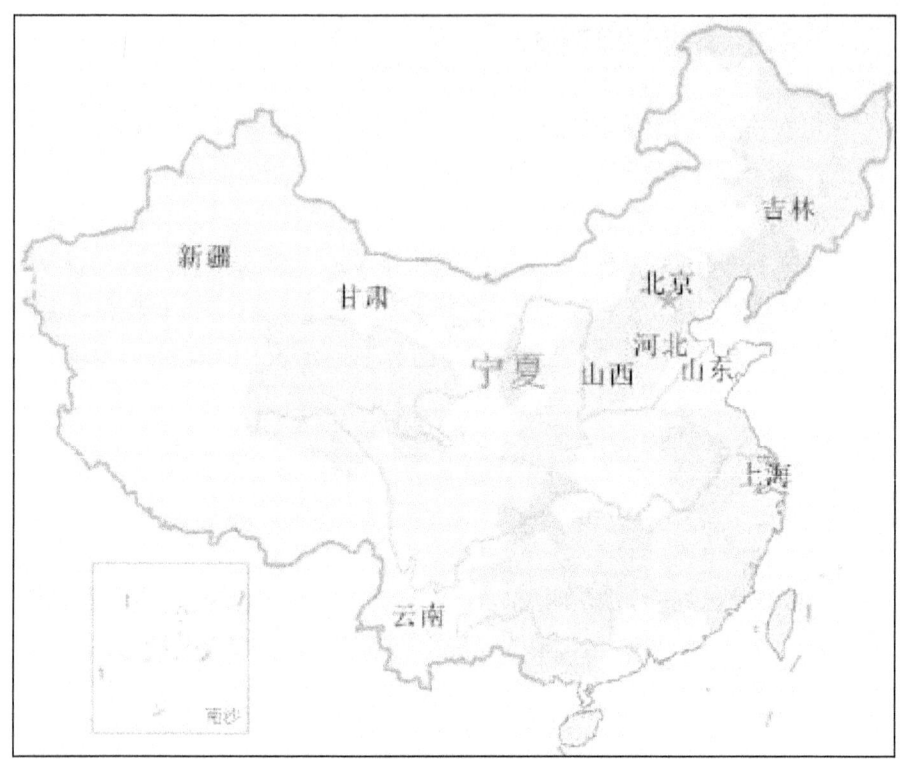

**中国主要葡萄酒产区地图**

5. **山西产区** - 位于北京以西,因怡园酒庄而闻名遐迩,该酒庄也是中国第一批使用酿酒葡萄出产广受褒奖、品质优良的葡萄酒的酒庄之一;

6. **甘肃产区** - 也位于中国中部,是宁夏以北一个更加凉爽的新兴葡萄栽培种植区;

7. **吉林产区** - 处在离北京遥远的东北方向,是个更加寒冷的地区,以冰葡萄酒而闻名;

8. **云南产区** - 中国最南的葡萄酒产区,靠近老挝和缅甸边境。虽然气候更为温暖,大多数葡萄园和酒庄都位于山区,最高海拔可达 9800 英尺。(Johnson & Robinson, 2013 年)。

中国其他一些地区也有种植酿酒葡萄，如陕西，天津以及全国其他的一些新兴地区。

## 中国的葡萄酒旅游

据世界旅游组织（UNWTO，2015)数据显示，在 2014 年，有 1.36 亿游客到访中国，位列北亚国家第一。有趣的是，中国同时也是世界上最大的旅游输出国，仅 2014 年，中国公民在世界各国的旅游消费总金额就高达 1650 亿美元（世界旅游组织，2015 年）。

谈到葡萄酒旅游，从到访中国葡萄酒产区的外国游客数量上来看，中国仍然处于起步阶段。部分原因可归结于目前的葡萄酒行业还是更多地着眼于吸引更多本国游客而非外国游客（Cao，2014）。尽管还是有部分旅游公司在宣传葡萄酒旅游，但实际上，国际访客仍需要获得签证或邀请函才能入境，这无疑是一大阻碍。尽管如此，还是有成千上万的中国游客参观了建立在中国各主要葡萄酒产区的宏伟酒庄并品酒。在这些酒庄中，有的走的是欧式城堡风格，有的则是传统中国堡垒式建筑。

*葡萄酒庄数量(中国)：625*
*葡萄酒庄数量(宁夏)：72*

**宁夏葡萄酒产区概况**

宁夏是中国 34 个省级行政区之一，自治区政府直接向北京中央政府汇报工作。其葡萄园位于中国中部地区，受山谷庇护，不会受来自贺兰山脉(最高峰可达 11000 英尺) 的寒冷北风侵扰，土壤主要成分是沙子和岩石，许多冲积扇从山上流下(类似于纳帕谷的冲积扇)，为葡萄生长营造了理想的环境。黄河流经葡萄园周围，穿越首府银川。葡萄园的平均海拔为 3000 英尺，大都建在冲积扇的平原地带，在贺兰山麓一带也有种植少量葡萄。（Cao，2014）。

宁夏地处北纬 38 度，属大陆性气候，夏季平均温度为 23 摄氏度(也可轻易达到 32 摄氏度)。冬季稍加艰难，有部分降雪，平均温度为零下 12 度。降雨量低，年均量从 8 到 27 英寸不等，但几乎所有的葡萄园都有滴灌系统。葡萄棚架系统主要采用长梢修枝的垂直枝条固定法。不允许葡萄藤过宽生长，在寒冷的冬天需要将它们填埋起来。目前，超过一半的葡萄藤是采用机械填埋（Cao，2014）

夏季的宁夏葡萄园

冬季的宁夏葡萄园

宁夏的首批葡萄园建于 1982，据宁夏官方报告称，截至 2014 年底，宁夏政府官员报告说，他们已经种植了约 39,000 公顷的葡萄藤，有 72 家酒庄投入了运营（Cao，2015）。宁夏葡萄酒产区的发展也得到了中央政府的大力支持，并获得了宁夏当地政府资助（Cao，2015）。目前，他们正在致力于吸引私人开发商和国际酒庄在该地区建立新的葡萄园和酒庄。

宁夏葡萄酒产区地图

由于宁夏还是一个相对新兴的葡萄酒产区，酒农们仍在不断试验探索最适合当地风土条件的葡萄品种。目前，他们种植了 40 个品种，其中主要有：

**赤霞珠** - 此地区的赤霞珠葡萄酒通常是中等酒体，呈现出不透明的浅宝石红色。果香扑鼻，有着浓郁的红黑浆果和香料的味道。赤霞珠以及赤霞珠混酿也是为当地酒庄斩获最多奖项的葡萄酒。

**梅洛** - 通常比赤霞珠颜色更深，有着令人垂涎的肉类风味和一些草本味道。

**蛇龙珠（亦称为中国赤霞珠）** - 该品种已被证实与佳美娜属同一品种，(Robinson，2012）。经常被用来酿制有着浓烈的草本气息，深色水果香气的葡萄酒，伴随着烟熏味和植物根茎味道，单宁较为涩口。

**意大利雷司令(贵人香)** - 花香与果香主导，带着热带菠萝的气息，酸度爽脆，酒体轻盈，亲和易饮。

**其他葡萄品种包括**：霞多丽，黑皮诺，品丽珠以及用来酿造冰葡萄酒的白威代尔。

## 宁夏的旅游产业

银川市是宁夏自治区首府，约有人口 200 万，距离北京和上海只有 2 小时飞行航程。每年，成千上万的国内游客都会前来参观各大旅游名胜，如西夏王陵、沙湖、贺兰山岩画、鼓楼，一百零八塔以及各大博物馆和寺庙。同时，银川还因每年 7 月举办的汽摩旅游节而闻名。

在葡萄酒旅游方面，宁夏政府还未开始积极宣传面向国际游客的酒庄游。在国内，他们更多地是采取"软着陆"的发展模式，目前尚未大力推广葡萄酒旅游。但对于身在银川的游客来说，如果提前预约，还是有机会去参观一些城堡酒庄的。另外，参加宁夏葡萄酒节也是一个不错的选择，内容包括有葡萄酒供应商出席的大型贸易展、葡萄酒品鉴、品尝当地美食及各类歌舞娱乐活动。

宁夏地区还以其独特的美食而闻名，比如用当季蔬果高汤烹制出的鲜嫩小羊肉就是其中一绝。该地区的另一大特产非一种小小的红色莓果莫属，即枸杞，通常人们会把枸杞干加到热汤中调味或是用来拌菜食用，有着类似小番茄干的味道。"今日中国"曾报道，宁夏有"五宝"，根据其颜色，被归为红，黄，白，黑，蓝五种，分别指枸杞、滩羊皮、甘草根、发菜和贺兰砚石（2014年，第1页）。发菜是一种藻类植物，因其柔软的质感和形如发丝的外观而得名。而贺兰砚石则是一种美丽的抛光花岗岩，呈深绿色或紫色，是中国三大著名防水砚石之一（China.org，2011）。

宁夏羊肉美食搭配葡萄　　　　　　贺兰晴雪酒庄"加贝兰"葡萄酒

**宁夏所面临的问题：优质葡萄酒产区地位未获全球认可**

宁夏第一个葡萄园是在 1982 年由玉泉营农场所建立，起初的目的是让当地工人获得就业机会，扩大该区农业生产。直到 2000 年底，宁夏作为世界级葡萄酒产区的概念才被提出。当时，曹局长和他的同事们正忙着为当地的经济增长出谋划策。在进行多次调研后，他们意识到宁夏的风土很适合种植酿酒葡萄。曹局长回忆起当时的情景：

"我们意识到宁夏位于中国葡萄园的"黄金地带"。研究表明，贺兰山东麓具有栽培高品质酿酒葡萄所需的一切自然条件，这包括充足的阳光，有利的温度区间，未污染的土壤，适当的降雨和灌溉。更重要的是，在此环境下培育出的芳香型葡萄具有极佳的酸甜平衡。

然而，问题在于如何使人们看到宁夏作为世界级葡萄酒产区的潜力。当时，大多数人并不相信中国可以生产高品质的葡萄酒。因为在 2000 年初，中国生产的大部分葡萄酒还是散装酒，国家对添加剂的使用和质量监控尚未出台明确法规。此外，中国人历来喝惯了米酒和高度白酒，大多数人也压根儿不知道好的葡萄酒尝起来是什么滋味。

另外一大挑战就是国际上的葡萄酒专家们从未听说过宁夏葡萄酒产区，自然难以得到全球认可。宁夏也亟需掌握世界一流的酿酒工艺，获得更多资金支持，开垦更多葡萄园，建立更多酒庄和建设与葡萄酒旅游相关的基础设施。一言以蔽之，努力从零打造一个世界级的葡萄酒胜地仍是宁夏所面临的艰巨任务。

**解决方案 --制定并落实产业发展策略，让宁夏成为全球优质葡萄酒产区，从而吸引游客**

值得庆幸的是，曹局长和他的团队赶上了一个好时机，因为中央政府正在鼓励发展新型农业项目，如葡萄酒生产，原因如下：首先，中国人更偏向将大米作为主食，而非是用来生产米酒；其次，他们担心高度数的白酒(通常 40 至 60 度)会对国民健康造成潜在的负面影响。此外，相较于许多农作物来说，葡萄藤的需水量更少，还可以在当前没有农业生产的地方进行种植。因此，葡萄种植和葡萄酒生产被视作朝阳产业。事实上，国营中粮集团旗下的长城牌葡萄酒品牌就是由中国政府大力资助的。

在中央政府的福泽下，宁夏政府决定为打造世界级的葡萄酒产区提供资金，并且期待在未来能有私人资本介入，为此，他们做了以下几件事情：

**1. 制定愿景和发展战略**

英国著名杂志《经济学人》的战略专家们曾多次指出，中国人富有远见，善于制定长期战略。该说法也在宁夏葡萄酒产业的愿景和战略规划中得到了充分印证。在 2000 年中期，宁夏政府制定出一个愿景：

在未来十年，使酒庄数量增长到 1,000 个以上，打造一个世界级的葡萄酒旅游胜地，在 2016 年实现接待大批中国游客，2017 年实现接待大量外国游客。还将开通一条沿途有宏伟的城堡、美丽的葡萄园的葡萄酒之路，开发一系列以健康、运动与休闲为主题的葡萄酒文化旅游产业链。最终将其打造成中国首屈一指的葡萄酒产区。

实现这个愿景需要采取三管齐下的战略：1) 发展人力资源人才，生产世界顶尖的葡萄酒; 2) 执行一套严格的质量控制体系，确保生产的葡萄酒达到世界级水准; 3) 创建国际标准的葡萄酒旅游基础设施并实施积极的区域品牌推广。为此，宁夏政府特别授权葡萄和花卉产业发展局负责各项管理工作并建立起一套完善的葡萄种植和葡萄酒生产监管体系。该局也是中国第一个负责区域葡萄酒行业管理的省级单位。作为中国首个创建严格的葡萄栽培和葡萄酒生产法规的产区，宁夏起到的带头作用不言而喻。

**2.获取资金支持**

在发展初期，宁夏政府提供了启动资金，让从业人员学习世界级的葡萄栽培以及酿酒技术，同时还邀请国际专家来建言献策，调研评估。慢慢的，随着宁夏多次展露光芒并开始斩获各类葡萄酒奖项，众多国内外企业都开始在该地区投资，其中就包括法国的酩悦·轩尼诗－路易·威登集团和保乐力加集团（见步骤 5）。

**3. 邀请全球葡萄酒专家并培训本地人才**

在实施战略初期，应集中拓展人力资源人才。因此，宁夏政府积极鼓励有心从事葡萄酒行业的当地人去波尔多学习葡萄栽培与酿酒技术。他们还聘请了来自法国，澳大利亚，美国，意大利和其他地区的诸多酿酒顾问，就如何改进葡萄栽培和酿酒环节提供建设性意见与指导。他们也邀请来自世界各地的教授和各领域专家就如何建设葡萄酒旅游基础设施和打响区域品牌提出实质性建议。

宁夏政府还与当地大学开展合作，建立了培训当地葡萄种植、葡萄酒酿造和葡萄酒旅游人才的教育计划。同时还与宁夏大学，宁夏理工学院，宁夏防治荒漠化研究所合作，并帮助成立了宁夏大学葡萄酒学院。此外，宁夏政府还为当地葡萄酒相关从业人员举办了一系列活动与各类教育项目，提供平台让他们与国外同行进行沟通交流，不断提升他们的技能水平。

**4. 建立质量评估指标**

对于宁夏产区发展来说，最重要的一个步骤很可能就是建立葡萄栽培和葡萄酒酿造的质量管控指标。他们鼓励葡萄的优栽优培，包括谨慎选择无病害的砧木和克隆品种，适当的葡萄园选址及设施的完善和滴灌系统的使用，鼓励使用有机/可持续的耕作方法。他们还制定了法规来限制高品质葡萄园的葡萄采收量：每亩收成不得超过 500 公斤，相当于每公顷 7.5 吨，或每英亩 3 吨。他们也创建了一个地理保护标识，命名为"贺兰山东麓葡萄酒产区"，也常简写为"宁夏葡萄酒产区"。

在酿酒法规方面，他们规定，一瓶葡萄酒中至少要有 75%的葡萄来自宁夏产区。此外，如果要在酒标上注明葡萄品种与年份，85% 的葡萄必须是同年采收的相同品种。这些规定与世界其他主要葡萄酒产区所建立的标准相似，并都由国际葡萄与葡萄酒组织所批准。

可能最令人印象深刻的就是酒庄分级制度的引入。效仿波尔多 1855 葡萄酒分级制度，宁夏将产区内的酒庄分为五级，并采用了更新的规则和每两年一评级的规定。要入选评级系统也是有门槛的，酒庄的葡萄酒产量必须达 4166 箱以上，并至少拥有 13 英亩的葡萄种植面积（Thach，2014）。

一个由葡萄栽培专家和教育专家所组成的国际葡萄酒专家组受邀对宁夏酒庄开展评估。葡萄园和葡萄酒的品质、旅游景点、餐饮住宿等条件都被考虑在内。在 2013 年的第一次评级中，共选出了 10 家五级酒庄。此后每两年会对酒庄进行重新评估，最终一些葡萄酒庄将被升级为四级庄、三级庄等。长远目标是实现五大级别的酒庄百家争鸣的盛景。然而，如果酒庄无法保持足够高的质量指标考核，他们也会面临降级或是被移除列级庄体系。Thach，2014）。

此外，宁夏政府还建立了一套葡萄酒旅游质量控制体系。为此，他们特别委托国际旅游与研究规划中心（CRTR）开展评估，对宁夏的旅游类酒庄进行排名（曹，2015）。

**5.鼓励金融投资**

为了实现建立一条宽阔的葡萄酒之路的愿景，宁夏政府邀请国内投资者建立新的配备有旅游设施的葡萄园和漂亮酒庄，这些设施包括品酒室、餐厅、住宿、游戏室、水疗中心等休闲场所。庆幸的是，他们开始实施该战略的阶段正值中国经济腾飞之际，因此许多投资者选择了该项目。

他们还践行了"贺兰山东麓葡萄酒产区保护条例"所列出的投资条款，要求每个投资者必须种植至少 13.3 公顷的无病害葡萄园，在获准修建城堡前至少得运作两年。同时也对投资者进行严格的评估，确保他们是真心想建立酒庄，杜绝不符合条件及抱着投机心理的开发商进入该地区。此外，他们还颁布条例，明文规定不符合标准的任何酒庄都将被拆除。新建城堡的最低投资额度为 2000 万元人民币（约 320 万美元）。当然，在中国，这类型的严格规定催生一个良好的投资契机，使投资者们愿意投钱进来并建立自己的专属城堡。

政府还鼓励投资者在宁夏建立葡萄酒生产设施。随着宁夏葡萄酒风土受到越来越多称赞以及一些早期酿造的宁夏葡萄酒开始荣获奖项，更多的投资者随之而来。法国人率先到达，酩悦·轩尼诗－路易·威登集团在当地建立了一个大型起泡酒厂，不久后保乐力加集团也接踵而至。此外，中国两家最大最知名的葡萄酒品牌张裕和长城也纷纷在宁夏设立酒厂。

政府也号召目前这一小批坐落在宁夏的酒厂扩大规模，着眼于高品质生产。为众多酒厂开展培训，以提高他们的各项技能，并协助企业发展营销和提供其他类型的支持。

**6. 打造高质量的国际品牌来吸引游客**

当宁夏正在建立质量指标的同时，他们开始了一个缓慢而谨慎的品牌策略。首先，宁夏方面精心挑选了一批国际记者和侍酒师到访该地品尝葡萄酒、参观酒厂、提供反馈意见、并让他们了解宁夏的葡萄酒发展愿景。然后这些专家们回国发表文章讲述自己在宁夏的见闻与体验。这些都对宁夏葡萄酒品牌的树立产生了积极影响。

几年来，宁夏葡萄酒一直参加中国的葡萄酒大赛，积极听取大赛评委的反馈，认识到不足，不断提升酒质。最终在 2011 年，他们决定将宁夏葡萄酒送到伦敦，参加由《醇鉴》杂志举办的世界葡萄酒大赛。包括他们自己在内的所有人都倍感惊讶，因为宁夏贺兰晴雪酒庄的葡萄酒荣获了 10 英镑以上波尔多红葡萄品种国际大奖。在该赛事中，共有超过 12000 款葡萄酒入围，而主办方仅授予了 25 个国际大奖。（Lechmere，2011）。获奖葡萄酒则是一款 2009 年的赤霞珠混酿，取名"加贝兰"，由酿酒顾问李德美先生和首席酿酒师张静女士合作完成，两人均在波尔多接受过相关专业培训。

张裕夏摩塞尔十五世酒庄，宁夏

该葡萄酒由赤霞珠，梅洛和蛇龙珠混酿而成，评委认为它"柔软，优雅，成熟却不招摇……余韵持久，单宁厚重"（Lechmere，2011，第 1 页）。"这一事件很快成为世界各地葡萄酒新闻头条，很快为宁夏葡萄酒产区创造了更多的正面新闻。更多的葡萄酒专家和记者想了解这个

产区，中国民众也为此振臂高呼，争相购买，2 万瓶的产量几乎在一夜之间被消耗一空

在 2012 年，宁夏政府又推出了一个"营销"计划，旨在引起全球对该地区的关注。他们创办了"酿酒师挑战赛"，在葡萄采收季的时候邀请世界各地的酿酒师前来酿酒并赢取免费宁夏游的机会。（Robinson，2014）这次活动吸引了许多国际媒体关注，此举也让世界看到，宁夏作为一个葡萄酒产区，是实实在在地倾注真心酿着好酒。从那之后，他们在2015 年又举办了该项挑战赛，并希望该赛事在未来一直持续下去。

贺兰晴雪酒庄，宁夏

## 7. 设计葡萄酒旅游基础设施

宁夏政府邀请了葡萄酒旅游专家就如何发展葡萄酒旅游基础设施提供建议。在几年的摸索过程中，他们开辟了一条葡萄酒之路，线路贯穿贺兰山麓大峡谷的葡萄园，并在地图上标明各大酒庄所处的位置。截

至 2014 年底，共有 72 家酒厂投入生产（Cao，2015），其中许多都设有品酒室、观光游览、餐饮住宿等旅游设施。

由于宁夏葡萄酒产区距离银川市区约有一个小时车程，他们也专注于在市区开发配套的旅游设施，为了迎接游客，他们翻新机场，树立起全新的欢迎标志。鼓励各大旅行社用面包车接送游客，从而发展国内市场的葡萄酒产区游。此外，他们还与银川市合作，与当地酒店和餐厅建立合作关系，方便游客们在市区有个落脚之处。银川市内的道路状况也得到了改善，市容也得到了美化，如增设喷泉，种植花草树木以及清除破旧建筑物。

宁夏政府还开始举办各类葡萄酒旅游活动，如 2012 年夏季开始的宁夏葡萄和葡萄酒节，如今仍是每年举办。他们还创办了一个国际葡萄酒博览会和葡萄酒设备技术展，吸引着国际葡萄酒专家、供应商和游客前来观展。

宁夏现在仍需要建设一个葡萄酒旅游网站并丰富营销手段，比如多语种的小册子和地图。他们还应该聘请一个专业的营销团队来帮助打造一个能代表宁夏产区的标志，开展相关宣传活动。不过，按照目前战略来看，宁夏旅游的国际化是在 2017 年，仍有足够时间来做好各项准备。

## 结果：葡萄酒旅游发展的最佳实践范例

宁夏可以被视作葡萄酒旅游发展的最佳实践范例，因为他们在短短十多年的时间里，已经卓有成效地从零建立起了一个葡萄酒产区。更重要的是，凭借着当地生产的高品质葡萄酒，他们树立起了响亮的名声。除了 09 年赢得国际葡萄酒大奖的加贝兰，许多其他的宁夏葡萄酒也大获褒奖。 比如由女性酿酒师高源酿制的葡萄酒，就受到了葡萄酒大师简希斯=罗宾逊的称赞。宁夏葡萄酒也给法国酒评家米歇尔·贝丹，切里-德梭和澳洲酒评家杰里米=奥利弗留下了深刻印象（Moselle，

2015）。其他知名的宁夏葡萄酒品牌还有巴克斯、兰一、类人首和圣路易-丁等。

据曹局长说，宁夏产区从 2000 年中期的少数葡萄酒庄发展到 2014 年底的 72 家葡萄酒庄，许多酒庄都拥有庞大宏伟的建筑。葡萄园面积也由 2006 年的 7,800 公顷增加到 2014 年的 39,000 公顷，目前生产的葡萄酒估值约 65 亿元人民币，相当于约 10 亿美元的收入（Cao，2015）。

根据国际专家组的评审，2013 年共有十家酒庄入选宁夏列级酒庄系统，均获五级庄地位。这些酒庄分别是：西夏王，志辉源石，贺兰晴雪，巴克斯，原哥，张裕摩塞尔十五世，兰一，禹皇，类人首和铖铖（Thach，2014）。

宁夏还实施了葡萄种植和葡萄酒酿造的质量控制体系，所以他们是中国唯一两个被邀请成为国际葡萄与葡萄酒组织观察员的葡萄酒产区之一。贺兰山东麓也获得了官方的地理标志认证，并被列入 2013 年出版的《世界葡萄酒地图》一书中。

宁夏产区的发展也是政府和社会组织(如大学、培训中心、私营企业)间合作的成果，不同实体间的合作被视作一个发展葡萄酒旅游的必要环节（Getz，2001）。

从结果来看，宁夏地区目前每年接待游客超过 165 万人次，消费金额达 140 亿元人民币（约合 22 亿美元）（曹，2015）。宁夏政府预计，在 7 至 11 年内会实现发展葡萄酒旅游的投资回报（Cao，2015）

**将来面临的问题**

尽管该地区发展迅速，但宁夏葡萄酒行业仍面临诸多挑战。其中一个问题就是外国葡萄酒的高供给量，这在一定程度上刺激了来自新旧世界生产国的知名葡萄酒以相对更低的价格流入中国。这无疑给国内葡萄酒生产商们造成了巨大压力。

另一个问题是，作为一个羽翼尚未丰满的年轻葡萄酒产区，宁夏正忙于努力实施其发展战略来提高葡萄种植水平和酿酒工艺。虽然宁夏在一定程度上取得了一些成功，但征途漫漫，仍需策马加鞭，不断前进。目前宁夏正在努力打造一条囊括世界级优质葡萄园开发、葡萄酒生产和营销/销售的综合产业链，从而确保整个葡萄酒行业的长期、健康地可持续性发展。

宁夏政府知道他们仍然需要关注的领域有：

***创建一个强大的地区品牌。***这包括明确区域标志的使用，向人们传递高品质的葡萄酒，健康，运动和休闲的信息。有必要探索新的营销模式，例如建立国际化的网站，充分利用社交媒体平台，以及在北上广等大城市的餐馆和葡萄酒专卖店中建立起宁夏葡萄酒的零售网络。此外，宁夏也需要继续参与国内外各大葡萄酒比赛以获取及时的产品反馈，并斩获越来越多的奖项。他们还期待建立起宁夏国际葡萄酒交易所和综合自由贸易区。

***强化宁夏"列级酒庄"管理制度。***宁夏葡萄酒行业的战略重心在于生产高品质的葡萄酒，所以应严格遵守宁夏"列级酒庄"制度中列出的每一项条款，将其落到实处。这包括每两年对葡萄园、葡萄酒和列级庄地位进行严格的国际评估。

***使葡萄酒旅游和葡萄酒文化更加便利化。***宁夏需要继续努力建设与葡萄酒旅游相关的基础设施，紧密围绕高品质葡萄酒、健康、运动和休闲的主题。为此，他们需要增加观光、美食、购物、娱乐等元素到旅游产品中。此外，他们还需要根据该主题来扩大葡萄园、酒庄、配套餐厅的规模并提供更多样化的休闲娱乐活动。

***继续发展技能，提供新就业机会。***宁夏政府意识到，需继续加强对葡萄种植、葡萄酒酿造、葡萄酒旅游、葡萄酒营销和相关葡萄酒工程建设从业人员的教育培训。

总之，宁夏并不满足于躺在过去的功劳簿上，反而对未来有着更宏伟的愿景。根据葡萄酒产业和文化走廊发展综合规划，到 2020 年，宁夏葡萄园将超过 66,000 公顷。除了建立一个葡萄文化中心，他们还计划建立三个生态酒城，十个风格迥异的葡萄酒主题城镇，使顶级城堡数量过百。他们的愿景是成为中国最大的酒庄集群，亚洲最大的葡萄酒产区，最终跻身世界顶级葡萄酒产区的行列。

—— **节选自《全球葡萄酒旅游的 12 种最佳实践》第四章**，Best Practices in Global Wine Tourism (2016), ISBN 9780971587069.

## 作者简介

### 张文晓

宁夏贺兰山东麓葡萄与葡萄酒国际联合会副秘书长，毕业于法国波尔多高等商学院葡萄酒专业，目前负责宁夏葡萄酒产区的营销策略制定和公共关系管理。

### 丽兹·塔什，葡萄酒大师

美国加州索诺玛州立大学特聘教授，兼任法国勃艮第商学院客座教授。负责教授本科和硕士阶段的葡萄酒工商管理课程。她钟情于葡萄酒，足迹遍布全球各大葡萄酒产区，发表了 120 多篇葡萄酒相关文章，出版了包括《Call of the Vine and Wine – A Global Business》在内的 6 部葡萄酒著作，并于 2011 年 5 月荣获"葡萄酒大师"头衔。

## 译者简介

### 战先勇

山东科技大学英美语言文学学士，法国勃艮第商学院葡萄酒管理硕士在读，曾实习于烟台威龙葡萄酒公司以及法国知名物流企业。葡萄酒达人，足迹遍布法国各大葡萄酒产区。
xianyongzhan@foxmail.com

### 邱继达

法国勃艮第商学院葡萄酒管理硕士在读，曾于法国世界报(Le Monde)和纽约联合国总部实习。目前为私人葡萄酒拍卖与收藏提供咨询。
jida.qiu@bsb-education.com

## 地图及图片来源

China Map courtesy of L. Thach, J. Qiu and X. Zhan

Ningxia Map courtesy of Ningxia Bureau of Grape and Floriculture Development

Photos courtesy of Ningxia Bureau of Grape and Floriculture Development and L. Thach

## 参考文献

Branigan, T. (2014). "China becomes biggest market for red wine, with 1.86bn bottles sold in 2013", *The Guardian. Retrieved on 8/11/15 at* http://www.theguardian.com/world/2014/jan/29/china-appetite-red-wine-market-boom/

Cao, K. (2014). Presentation by Kailong Cao at International Wine Tourism Seminar. Yinchuan, China. December 2014

Cao, K. (2015). Presentation by Kailong Cao to media. Yinchuan, China. March 2015

Changyu.com (2014). Website of Changyu. Retrieved on 8/12/15 at http://www.changyu.com.cn:8189/

China Today. (2014). China City and Province: Ningxia Hui Autonomous Region. *Chinatoday.com*. Retrieved on 8/18/15 at http://www.chinatoday.com/city/ningxia.htm

China.org (2011). Helan Today. *China.org website*. Retrieved on 8/17/15 at http://www.china.org.cn/travel/Ningxia/2011-01/11/content_21715104.htm.

ChinaCulture.org. (2003). Introduction to the oldest wine. *ChinaNewsDaily.com*. Retrieved on 8/12/15 at http://www.chinaculture.org/gb/en_curiosity/2005-01/26/content_65456.htm.

Clove Garden. (n.d.). Fat Choy - Black Moss. *Clove Garden Blog*. Retrieved on 8/17/15 at http://www.clovegarden.com/ingred/al_fatchz.html

Gastin, D. (2014). Understanding the China Syndrome. *Winestate Annual 2015*. Dec. 17, 2014.

Getz. D. (2001). *Explore Wine Tourism: Management, Development & Destinations*. NY: Cognizant Communications

Jiang Lu, (2015). Grape Wine Today in China. Presentation at UC Davis from China Agricultural University in Beijing. 3/16/15. Retrieved on 8/12/15 at http://confucius.ucdavis.edu/local_resources/js/JIangLU_Grape%20Wine%20Today%20in%20China%203-26%20UC%20Davis.pdf

Johnson, H & Robinson, J. (2013). "China." Chapter in 7th edition of

*The World Wine Atlas*. London: Octopus Publishing Co.

Lawrence, J. (2012). China to drink more white wine, says study. *Decanter*. Retrieved on 8/12/15 at http://www.decanter.com/wine-news/chinese-to-drink-more-white-wine-study-predicts-28569/

Lechmere, A. (2011). Chinese wine wins top honor at Decanter World Wine Awards. *Decanter*, Sept. 8, 2011. Retrieved on 8/17/15 at http://www.decanter.com/wine-news/chinese-wine-wins-top-honour-at- decanter-world-wine-awards-36689/.

Lyons, W. (2013). "Indulge in China's Latest Export". *Wall Street Journal*. Retrieved on 8/12/15 at http://www.wsj.com/articles/SB10001424127887323296504578396131833363780

Moselle, M. (2015). Ningxia Winemaker's Contest to shine spotlight on rising Chinese region. *Food & Drink*. Retrieved on 8/18/15 at http://www.scmp.com/lifestyle/food-drink/article/1831690/ningxia- winemakers-contest-shine-spotlight-rising-chinese.

OIV (2014). State of World Vitiviniculture situation. Paper presented at *37th World Congress of Vine and Wine*. Mendoza, Argentina. Nov. 10, 2014.

Robinson, J. (2012). Changyu, Cabernet Gernischt Blend 2011 Ningxia. *JancisRobinson.com*. Retrieved on 8/17/15 at http://www.jancisrobinson.com/articles/changyu-cabernet-gernischt-blend-2011-ningxia

Robinson, J. (2012a). Emma Gao - a story of wine today. *JancisRobinson.com*. http://www.jancisrobinson.com/articles/emma-gao-a-story-of-wine-today

Robinson, J. (2014). Australian triumphs in Ningxia. *JancisRobinson.com*. Retrieved on 8/17/15 at http://www.jancisrobinson.com/articles/australian-triumphs-in-ningxia

StatOIV (2014). *StatOIV Extracts*. Retrieved on 8/12/15 at http://www.oiv.int/oiv/info/enstatoivextracts2

Sylvia Wu, (2014). "Ningxia wine region: We've got your back, says the government", *Decanter- China*. Retrieved on 8/11/15 at https://www.decanterchina.com/en/?article=894

Thach, L. (2009). The Enchanting City of Turpan and the Uyghurs. *Wine Travel Stories Blog*. Retrieved on 8/12/15 at http://winetravelstories.blogspot.com/2009/09/enchanting-city-of-turpan-and-uyghurs.html

Thach, L. (2013). A Snapshot of wineries and Vineyards in the Ningxia Wine Region of China. *Wine Travel Stories Blog*. Retrieved on 8/12/15 at http://winetravelstories.blogspot.com/2013/12/a-snapshot-of- wineries-and-vineyards-in.html

Thach, L. (2014). "Chinese Wine Region Establishes Classification

Modeled on Bordeaux's." *Wine Spectator,* Jan. 30, 2014. Retrieved on 8/11/15 at http://www.winespectator.com/webfeature/show/id/49539

The Economist. (2014). Playing the Long Game. *The Economist Intelligence Unit.* Retrieved on 8/17/15 at http://www.economistinsights.com/energy/analysis/playing-long-game

Wine China. (2014). Inside Industry. *Winechina.com – website of the China Alcoholic Drinks Association.* Retrieved on 8/18/15 at http://www.winechina.com/template/NewsEnSearch.aspx?caten=Inside%20Industry&caten2=China%20Wine%20Region

Zhuan Ti. (2014). "Ningxia Nurtures Big Plans For Wine", *Washington Post.* Retrieved on 8/11/15 at http://chinawatch.washingtonpost.com/2014/08/ningxia_nurtures_big_plans_for_wine/

*English Version*
Chapter Four in Best Practices in Global Wine Tourism:
15 Case Studies from Around the World
Edited by Dr. Liz Thach, MW and Dr. Steve Charters, MW
Published by Miranda Press, New York, 2016. ISBN: 9780971587069

# Building a Wine Destination from Scratch in Ningxia, China

Wenxiao Zhang & Liz Thach
*Grape & Floriculture Bureau, Ningxia, China & Sonoma State University, California, USA*

The highest peak of the Helan Mountains rose over 3500 meters, towering over the irrigated plain that was home to the more than 39,000 vineyard hectares in the Ningxia wine region, located in Central China. Glancing up, Mr. Kailong Cao, Director of the Bureau of Grape and Floriculture Development for the province, could see a dusting of white snow on the far peaks on this sunny December morning.

In front of him, moving slowly across the sandy plain that was blessed with the alluvial soil washed down from the Helan Mountains, were six large bulldozers creating more vineyards for the burgeoning Ningxia wine region. Mr. Cao smiled as he realized his dreams of creating a world-class wine tourism destination were coming true. He remembered twenty years ago when there was nothing here but vacant land. Now this valley, situated at 38 degrees north latitude, the same as Napa Valley, was creating some of China's best wines including *Jai Bei Lan*, which won the *Decanter World Wine Awards* in 2011.

Mr. Cao turned to address the group of international journalists standing behind him snapping photographs and scribbling in their note pads. His breath was visible in the frosty air as he described in Chinese all of the progress they had made in the last several years. His translator expertly relayed his message in English and French, and then the visitors began to ask questions. Mr. Cao smiled, delighted to describe the journey that had allowed him and his team to create a wine destination in Central China from scratch.

## OVERVIEW OF THE CHINESE WINE INDUSTRY

China has been producing wine since 1600 BC, according to scientists who discovered ancient pottery vessels in the Henan Province, with organic residue revealing a fermented beverage of rice, honey and fruit (China Culture, 2003). However, the term "wine" in Chinese is "*jiu*," and refers to any type of alcoholic beverage. It is important to clarify grape wine by using the term "*putaojui*." For centuries, rice wine has been much more popular in China than wine made from grapes, though China does have its own indigenous grape varieties - *vitis amurensis.*

Wine produced from *vitis vinifera* grape varieties was first made in China in the 1890's in the town of Yantai in the Shandong Province. It was here that Zhang Bishi, a Chinese businessman and diplomat who traveled frequently overseas, decided to open the first large-scale winery and called it Changyu Pioneer Wine Company (Lyons, 2013). Importing wine grape cuttings from Europe, he found that many did not survive, so he grafted them to the native Chinese rootstock and had much more success. Eventually, he began winning medals for his wines at international competitions. Today Changyu is one of the largest wineries in China, with eight massive chateaux in various regions of the country, as well as international holdings (Changyu.com, 2014).

Eventually, during the mid to late 1900's other grape wine establishments began to appear in China, including the giant COFCO winery operated by the Chinese government, which produces the famous *Great Wall* wine brand. According to the StatOIV (2014), China's grape vineyards grew from 300,000 hectares in 2000 to 560,000 hectares by 2011, and their world ranking was fifth largest in wine production in 2012 (OIV, 2014). The latest report on the number of wineries in China was 625 (Gastin, 2014).

**Major Wine Varietals in China**

According to Jiang Lu (2015), a professor at the China Agriculture University in Beijing, 80% of the grapes grown in China are table grapes, with 15% used as wine grapes and 5% for raisins. He cites that major grape varietals planted in China include Cabernet Sauvignon at 49.6%, Carmenere at 9.6% (also referred to as Chinese Gernischt), Merlot at 8.5%, and Syrah and Chardonnay, both at less than 2%. More red wine is sold in China than white wine, primarily because the color red is thought to bring good luck, but some sources report that white wine in gaining in popularity in China (Lawrence, 2012).

**Eight Major Wine Regions of China**

Currently there are eight major wine regions in China (Johnson & Robinson, 2013):

1) **Shandong** – the oldest wine-producing region with the largest number of wineries. Located on a peninsula that juts out into the Yellow Sea, it has a more moderate climate, but often has high humidity that causes mildew problems for wine grape production.

2) **Xinjiang** – the second largest grape producing region, but with a large percentage of table grapes as well as some wine grapes. Located to the far west of China, the region is dry and arid, but has very cold winters that require the vines to be buried underground to protect them. A primarily Muslim area of China, it is part of the original Silk Trail and has towns such as Turpan where they have been producing wine since 300 B.C. (Thach, 2009).

3) **Ningxia** – located in central China near the Helan Mountain range, Ningxia is known for its dry, sunny climate and production of high quality wines. Though it is still often cold enough to require the vines be buried in the winter, the climate is friendlier to producing healthy grapes, and the alluvial soils and Yellow River flowing nearby provide positive conditions for wine grapes.

4) **Hebei** – located just outside the major city of Beijing, Hebei is home to some very large wineries. It has the added advantage of luring many tourists due to its proximity to the Great Wall of China and the Summer Palace.

*Map of Major Chinese Wine Regions*

5) **Shanxi** – located west of Beijing, Shanxi is famous for the headquarters of Grace Winery, which was one of the first wineries in China to achieve acclaim for its high quality wines produced with *vitis vinifera* grapes.
6) **Gansu** – also located in central China, Gansu is a newer viticulture area in a cooler location north of Ningxia.
7) **Jilin** – located to the far northeast of Beijing, Jilin is a much cooler area renowned for its ice wines.
8) **Yunnan** – also referred to as Hunnan, is the most southern wine region of China close to the borders of Laos and Burma. Though a warmer region, most of the vineyards and wineries are located in the mountains at altitudes of up to 9800 feet (Johnson & Robinson, 2013).

There are some other regions in China also growing wine grapes, such as Shaanxi (not to be confused with Shanxi) and Tianjin near Beijing, as well as a few emerging areas in others parts of the country.

**Wine Tourism in China**

According to the World Tourism Organization (UNWTO, 2015), China ranked first in most visited countries in North Asia with 136 million tourists visiting in 2014. Interestingly China was also the world's top tourism source, in that many Chinese citizens visited multiple countries around the world to spend a total of $165 billion on tourist activities outside of China in 2014 (UNWTO, 2015).

In terms of wine tourism, China is still in its infancy regarding international tourists visiting Chinese wine regions. Part of this has to do with the fact that the industry is focused more on attracting national Chinese tourists than non-nationals (Cao, 2014). Though there are a few tour companies that advertise wine tours, the fact that international visitors are still required to obtain a visa, and often an invitation letter, makes this more challenging. Despite this fact, thousands of Chinese tourists visit the amazing wine chateaux and tasting rooms that have been constructed in some of the major Chinese wine regions. Some look like European castles, whereas others use traditional Chinese fortress architecture.

## OVERVIEW OF THE NINGXIA WINE REGION

Ningxia is one of 34 provincial level administrative regions in China, and has its own government that reports to the central Chinese government in Beijing. Located in Central China, Ningxia vineyards lie in a protected valley and are sheltered from the cold Northern winds by the Helan Mountains, that rise over 11,000 feet tall at their highest peak. The soil consists primarily of sand and rocks, with many alluvial fans flowing down the sides of the mountain to form an ideal grape growing foundation, similar to the alluvial fans found in Napa Valley. The Yellow River flows near the vineyards and through the nearby capital city of Yinchuan. Elevation of the vineyards averages 3,000 feet, with most vines established on the flatter plains of the alluvial fans, but a few planted on the foothills of the Helan Mountains (Cao, 2014).

| # of Wineries in China | 625 |
| --- | --- |
| # of Wineries in Ningxia | 72 |

Situated at 38 degrees north latitude, the climate is Continental with average summer highs of 74 F, though it can easily reach into the 90's F. Winters can be harsh with some snow and average temperatures of 10 F. Rainfall is low, ranging from 8 to 27 inches per year, but almost all vineyards have drip irrigation. The trellis system is primarily vertical shoot positioning (VSP) with cane pruning. The trunks of the vines are not allowed to grow very wide, because they must be buried during the cold winters. Currently more than 50% of the vines are buried mechanically (Cao, 2014).

The first vineyards were planted in 1982, and by the end of 2014 Ningxia government officials reported that they had planted roughly 39,000 hectares of vines, and have 72 wineries in operation (Cao, 2015). Expansion and promotion of Ningxia as a wine region has been encouraged by the Chinese central government, and funded by the Ningxia government (Cao, 2015). Currently, they are engaged in an ongoing effort to attract private developers and international wineries to establish new vineyards and wineries in the region.

Interestingly, the term for a Chinese acre is mu, and equals 1/15$^{th}$ of a hectare. Therefore 39,000 hectares would be roughly equivalent to 585,000 mu. Since a hectare equals 2.47 acres, this would be equivalent to 96,330 acres.

*Winter Vineyard in Ningxia*

As Ningxia is a relatively new wine region, growers are still experimenting to determine the best type of varietals to cultivate in their climate. Therefore, they have currently planted 40 varieties, but the main ones are:
- *Cabernet Sauvignon* – the cabernets from this region are medium-bodied with a light ruby non-opaque color. They are fruit forward with concentrated red and black berry flavors and spices. Ningxia wineries have won the most awards on their cabernet sauvignon and cab blends.
- *Merlot* – often darker in color than the cabs, with savory meaty flavors and some herbal components.
- *Chinese Gernischt* (also called Chinese Cabernet) - this

varietal has been proven to be the same as Carmenere (Robinson, 2012). In China, it seems to produce wines that have a strong herbal, almost green note with dark, smoky fruit and astringent tannins.
- *Italian Riesling* – floral, fruity with some tropical notes of pineapple producing light and approachable wines with a crisp acidity.
- Other grape varietals include: chardonnay, pinot noir, cabernet franc, and vidal blanc; the latter of which is used to make ice wines.

**Tourism in Ningxia**

The capital of Ningxia is Yinchuan, a city of around 2 million people. It is located only 2 hours by plane from both Beijing and Shanghai, and receives thousands of Chinese tourists each year who come to visit some of its famous tourist sites. These include the Xia Tombs, Sand Lake, Helanshan Rock Paintings, the Drum Tower, the 108 Dagobas, and several other museums and temples. Yinchuan is also famous for the Automobile and Motorcycle Tourism Festival that is held every July.

In terms of wine tourism, the Ningxia government has not yet started to actively promote visits to the wineries for international tourists. Domestically, Ningxia is using more of a "soft launch approach," with no strong promotion of wine tourism at this time. Yet domestic tourists who arrive in Yinchuan have the opportunity to visit some of the chateaux if they make appointments in advance. They may also be able to attend the Ningxia Grape & Wine Festival, which includes a large trade show with wine suppliers, wine tastings, excellent food, and entertainment such as dancers and singers.

*Ningxia Lamb Dish*            *Jiabeilan Wine*

The Ningxia region is also known for its unique cuisine, including tender young lamb cooked in broth, organic vegetables, and fresh fruit in season. Another specialty of the region is the Chinese wolfberry, which is a small red berry, usually served dry and added to soups and salads. It has a taste that is similar to dried tomatoes. According to China Today, "Ningxia is known for five specialties or treasures, described as "red, yellow, white, black, and blue" because of their respective colors." These are the "wolfberry, sheep fur, liquorice root, facai, and Helan stone (2014, p. 1)." Facai is a moss that is also known as the "hair vegetable," because it has a soft texture like vermicelli and the appearance of black hair (Clove Garden, n.d.). The special stone of the Helan Mountains is a beautiful polished granite, which is often dark green and/or purple in color, and is one of three famous ink stones in China that are water resistant (China.org, 2011).

*Map of the Ningxia Wine Region*

## THE PROBLEM: NO GLOBAL RECOGNITION AS A FINE WINE GROWING REGION

Even though the first vineyards were planted in Ningxia in 1982 by Yu Quanying Farm as a means to provide employment opportunities for local workers and to expand the agriculture business of the region, it wasn't until the late 2000's that the concept of Ningxia as a world class wine region came into being. At that time, Mr. Cao and his staff at the Bureau of Grape and Floriculture Development were trying to identify strategic growth businesses for the region. After conducting some studies they realized that the terroir was ideally suited to wine grapes. Mr. Cao reflected on this discovery:

> *"We realized we were located in a "golden zone" for vineyards in China. Our studies showed that the east foothill of Helan Mountain has all the natural conditions needed for premier wine grape cultivation. This includes adequate sunlight and favorable temperature range, pollution-free soil, decent rainfall and irrigation. Even more important, we realized that the environment produces aromatic grapes with balanced sugar and acid levels."*

The problem, however, was how to gain recognition that Ningxia could be a world-class wine region. At the time, most people didn't think that China could ever produce high quality wine. For the most part, this perception was justified in the early 2000's, because much of the wine that was produced in China was bulk wine with no clear regulations on additives or quality. Also, because the Chinese population had a long history with rice wine and high alcohol *baijiu*, most people didn't know how good wine was supposed to taste.

To complicate the problem further, international wine experts had never heard of the Ningxia wine region, so there was no global recognition. Other issues had to do with the need to develop world-class winemaking skills, obtain more financial backing, plant more vineyards, build wineries, and develop a wine tourism infrastructure. Taken altogether, Ningxia had the daunting task of trying to develop a world-class wine destination from scratch.

# THE SOLUTION: DEVELOP STRATEGY TO BECOME A HIGH QUALITY GLOBAL WINE REGION TO ATTRACT TOURISTS

Fortunately, the timing was good for Mr. Cao and his staff, because the Chinese central government in Beijing was encouraging new agriculture projects, such as wine grape production, for several reasons. The first was that they preferred to use rice as a food product instead of a means to produce rice wine, and secondly they were concerned about the high alcohol content of *baijiu*, often 40 to 60 proof, and the potential negative impact it had on health. Additionally, wine grapes needed less water than many other crops and could be grown in places where there was currently no agriculture. Therefore viticulture and wine production was viewed positively at the time. Indeed the Chinese government invested in the Great Wall wine brand as part of their state run China National Cereals, Oils and Foodstuffs Corporation, or COFCO.

With the blessings of the central government, the Ningxia government decided to fund the development of a world-class wine region, with the expectation that private funding would also be solicited in the future. In order to do this, they implemented the following steps.

## Step One: Develop a Vision & Strategy

Strategy experts have frequently pointed to China as being an expert at visionary thinking and long-term strategy (The Economist, 2014), and in the case of the Ningxia wine region vision and strategy, this seems to hold true. In the mid 2000's the Ningxia government created a vision to:

> *Expand to more than 1,000 wineries in the next decade, and create a world-class wine tourism destination for Chinese tourists by 2016 and international tourists by 2017. The region will have a wine route with great chateaux, vineyards, and a chain of wine and cultural tourism experience focusing on Health, Sport and Relaxation. It will be renowned as the premier wine-growing region of China.*

The strategy to implement the vision included a three-pronged approach to 1) develop human resource talent to produce world-class wine; 2) execute a quality control system to ensure world-class wine; and 3) create a world-class wine tourism infrastructure and positive regional branding to promote it.

In order to accomplish this, the Ningxia government appointed the Bureau of Grape and Floriculture Development to manage the process and set up a regulatory system for grape and wine production. This made the Bureau the first provincial level institution in China to be charged with the management of a regional wine industry. It also highlighted Ningxia as the first region in China to create stringent regulations for local viticulture and wine quality production.

**Step Two: Obtain Financial Backing**

In the beginning the Ningxia government provided the initial funding to train employees in world-class viticulture techniques and wine production, as well as to provide money to bring in international experts to advise and evaluate. However, as Ningxia started to gain more positive press with articles and wine awards, both domestic and foreign enterprises, such as French conglomerates LVMH and Pernod Ricard, were encouraged to invest in the region (see step 5).

## Step Three: Invite Global Wine Experts and Train Locals

During the early implementation of the strategy, the main focus was on the development of human resource talent. Therefore the Ningxia government encouraged interested locals in studying viticulture and winemaking in Bordeaux. They also hired many winemaking consultants from France, Australia, the USA, Italy, and other regions to provide advice on what they could do to improve viticulture and winemaking practices. They invited professors and other experts from around the world to make recommendations on how to implement a wine tourism infrastructure and build a regional brand.

The Ningxia government also partnered with local universities to establish educational programs to train locals in viticulture, winemaking, and wine tourism. They worked with Ningxia University, Ningxia Polytechnic School, the Ningxia Institute of Prevention and Control of Desertification, and helped to establish the Wine School of Ningxia University. In addition, the Ningxia government carried out a series of activities and educational events for local wine industry participants to communicate with their foreign counterparts in order to improve their skill levels.

## Step Four: Establish Quality Metrics

Probably one of the most important steps Ningxia took was to establish quality control metrics for viticulture and wine. They began by encouraging best practices in viticulture, including careful rootstock and clone selection with no disease, proper vineyard set-up and installation, the use of drip irrigation, and encouragement to use organic and/or sustainable farming practices. They also established regulations on the amount of grapes that could be harvested from a high quality vineyard, as no more than 500kg per mu. This equates to 7.5 tons per hectare, or 3 tons per acre. They created a Geographical Indicator and named the region "Helan Mountain's East Foothill Wine Region", which is frequently shortened to "Ningxia Wine Region."

In terms of winemaking regulations, they established that at least 75% of the grapes in a bottle must be grown in the Ningxia region. In addition, 85% must be of the same variety and vintage in order to list varietal and vintage on the bottle. These standards are similar to those established by other major wine regions of the world, and sanctioned by the OIV.

Probably most impressive was the introduction of a winery classification system. Modeled on the Bordeaux 1855 Classification, but with updated rules and a required renewal every two years, it ranks wineries into five levels. In order to be considered, wineries must make at least 4,166 cases and farm at least 13 acres of vineyards (Thach, 2014).

An international group of wine experts including viticulture specialists and educators is brought in to evaluate the wineries, which Ningxia refers to as chateaux. Quality of vineyards, wine, and tourist attractions, including restaurants and lodging, are judged. During the first year of implementation in 2013, the judges selected 10 wineries as fifth-growths. Every two years wineries will be re-evaluated and eventually some will be promoted to fourth growth, third growth, etc. The long-term goal is that there will be chateaux classified in all five levels. Wineries can also be demoted or dropped from the classification if they do not maintain high enough quality levels (Thach, 2014).

Further, the Ningxia government established a quality control system for wine tourism. To do so they commissioned the International Center for Recreation and Tourism Research (CRTR) to evaluate the ranking of tourism wineries in Ningxia.

**Step Five: Encourage Financial Investment**

In order to implement their vision of a vast wine route, the Ningxia government invited domestic investors to establish new vineyards and great chateaux with tourist facilities, such as tasting rooms, restaurants, lodging, game rooms, spas, and other appealing venues. Fortunately they launched this phase of the strategy implementation when the economy was booming in China, and therefore many wealthy people invested in the project.

They also established conditions listed in the Regulations on Conservation of Helan Mountain's East Foothill Wine Region. These required that each investor plant a virus free vineyard of at least 13.3 hectares, and that it be in operation at least two years before they were allowed to build a chateau. Investors were strictly evaluated to ensure they were serious about creating wineries, and to prevent unqualified and speculative transactions-motivated developers from entering the region. Additionally, they set up regulations stating that any chateau not meeting the standard of the wine region would be removed. The minimum investment for a newly constructed chateau was set at RMB 20 million yuan (about USD 3.2 million). Naturally, in China, these types of strict regulations created a prestige buying opportunity, and spawned more desire on the part of the wealthy to buy into the project and build their own chateau.

Foreign investors were also encouraged to establish production facilities in Ningxia, and once word spread about the positive aspects of the terroir and awards on some of the early wines, this soon attracted others. The French were the first to arrive, with LVMH establishing a large sparkling production facility, and Pernod-Ricard following soon after. In addition, two of the largest and most famous wine brands of China set-up operations in Ningxia, namely Changyu and Great Wall.

Finally, the handful of regional wineries that had already existed within Ningxia were encouraged to expand and focus on high-quality production. Many were given educational opportunities to enhance their skills sets, and assistance with marketing and other types of support.

*Chateau Changyu Moser XV in Ningxia*

## Step Six: Build a High Quality Global Brand to Attract Tourists

At the same time as Ningxia was engaged in establishing their quality metrics, they started a slow and subtle branding strategy. It began by inviting handpicked international journalists and sommeliers to the region to taste wines, visit wineries, provide feedback, and learn about the regional wine vision. These experts returned home and published articles, which created some positive press.

Ningxia also entered their wines in Chinese competitions for several years, learning about needed improvements from the judge's feedback. Eventually in 2011, they decided to submit wines into the *Decanter World Wine Awards* competition in London. They were just as surprised as the rest of the world when Chateau Helan Qingxue won the Red Bordeaux Varietal Over £10 International Trophy. Out of over 12,000 wines entered, only 25 international trophies are awarded at this competition (Lechmere, 2011). The wine was a 2009 Cabernet blend called Jiabeilan. It was made by two Chinese winemakers both trained in Bordeaux: male consulting winemaker, Li Demei, and female head winemaker, Zhang Jing.

The wine was a blend of cabernet sauvignon, merlot and cabernet gernicht (carmenere), and judges described it as "supple, graceful and ripe but not flashy…, excellent length and four-square tannins (Lechmere, 2011, p. 1)." This single event made headlines around the world, and immediately created even more positive press for the Ningxia wine region. More professional wine experts and journalists wanted to learn about the area, and Chinese nationals were thrilled that a Chinese wine had garnered such acclaim. Though 20,000 bottles had been produced, it nearly sold out overnight as many people in China clamored to purchase a bottle.

Then in 2012, the Ningxia government introduced another "marketing" scheme designed to bring global attention to the region. They established the "Winemaker's Challenge," in which winemakers from around the world were invited to apply to win a free trip to Ningxia to make wine during harvest (Robinson, 2014). This event received much international press, and helped put Ningxia on the world stage as a winemaking region that was serious about making good wine. Since that time, they have repeated the Winemaker's Challenge in 2015, and hope to do so again in the future.

**Step Seven: Design a Wine Tourism Infrastructure**

The Ningxia government invited experts in wine tourism to advise them on how to develop a wine tourism infrastructure. Over the course of several years, they created a wine route through the vineyards in the large valley that lay at the base of the Helan Mountains, and created a map showing where wineries were located. By the end of 2014, there were a total of 72 wineries in production (Cao, 2015), with many having tourist facilities such as tasting rooms, tours, restaurants, and lodging.

Because the wine region is located about an hour drive from the city of Yinchuan, they also focused on developing tourist support systems there as well. The airport was spruced up for visitors, and new welcome signs were erected. Tour companies with vans to carry visitors were encouraged to develop tours of the wine region for domestic tourists. In addition, they worked with the city of Yinchuan to develop partnerships with local hotels and restaurants so that visitors would have a place to stay in town. Roads in the town of Yinchuan were improved, along with a beautification scheme, such as adding fountains, trees, and flowers, and removing rundown buildings.

The Ningxia government also began organizing wine tourism events, such as the Ningxia Grape and Wine Festival that was started in the summer of 2012, and has been offered every year since. They also host an International Wine Expo and Site Vinitech that brings in international wine experts, suppliers, and tourists.

They still need to develop a wine tourism website and other marketing materials, such as brochures and maps, to be available in multiple languages. In addition, they will need to hire a professional marketing team to develop a logo and advertising campaign. However, since the strategy is to open Ningxia to international tourist in 2017, there is still time to accomplish this.

## RESULTS AND BEST PRACTICE IMPLICATIONS

Ningxia can be considered a best practice in wine tourism because they effectively built a wine region from scratch in a little over a decade. More importantly, they were able to achieve very positive press based on the high quality of their wines. Not only did the 2009 Jaibelan win the International Trophy for best Red Bordeaux Varietal Over £10, many of the wines from other Ningxia wineries have also received glowing reviews. Silver Heights wines, produced by female winemaker, Emma Gao, have received excellent reviews from Jancis Robinson (2012a), and Michel Bettane, Thierry Desseauve and Jeremy Oliver are also impressed with Ningxia wines (Moselle, 2015). Other well perceived Ningxia wine brands include Bacchus, Lanny, Leirenshou, and St. Louis Ding.

The Ningxia wine region grew from a handful of wineries in the mid 2000's to 72 wineries by the end of 2014, with many having very large and impressive architecture. The size of the vineyard land has also increased from 7,800 hectares in 2006 to over 39,000 hectares in 2014, and currently produces wine that is evaluated to be worth 6.5 billion yuan, equating to around one billion US dollars in revenues (Cao, 2015).

The Ningxia winery classification system has resulted in ten wineries earning fifth-growth status in the 2013, as determined by a panel of international experts. These wineries are: Xixia King, Chateaux Yuanshi, Helan Qingxue, Bacchus, Yuange, Changyu Moser XV, Lanyi, Yuhuang, Leirenshou, and Chengcheng (Thach, 2014).

Ningxia has also implemented quality control systems for viticulture and winemaking. Because of this, they are one of only two wine regions in China that have been invited to become an OIV observer. They were also recognized by the Chinese Committee of National Geography with their Geographic Indicator of the East Foothill of Helan Mountains, which was also listed in *The World Atlas of Wine* in 2013.

The region has also illustrated a pattern of cooperation between government, social organizations, such as universities and training centers, and private enterprises. Collaboration between different entities is considered to be one of the hallmarks of best practice wine tourism (Getz, 2001).

In terms of results, the Ningxia region now receives over 1.65 million tourists each year, which spent an estimated 14 billion yuan ($2.2 billion US dollars) in Ningxia in 2014 (Cao, 2015). The Ningxia government estimates it will see a financial return on their investment in developing their wine industry within 7 to 11 years (Cao, 2015).

## FUTURE ISSUES

Despite the rapid advancement of the region, the Ningxia wine industry still faces many challenges. One issue is the high level of wine supply outside of China, which has inspired well-known wines from the Old and New World wine producing countries to flow into China at relatively low prices. This puts great pressure on domestic Chinese wine producers.

Another issue has to do with the fact that Ningxia is still a young wine region, and is working hard to implement their strategy to increased quality in vineyards and wine production. Though they have succeeded to some extent, they still need to strive for continuous improvement. They are working to create an integrated industrial chain comprised of world-class vineyard development, wine production, and marketing/sales to ensure long-term sustainability of the wine industry.

Areas on which the Ningxia government knows they still need to focus are:

- **Creating a strong brand for the region.** This includes clarification of the regional logo and emphasis on high quality wine, health, sport, and relaxation as the main messages. There is a need to explore new ways of marketing such as launching an international website, utilizing social media, and establishing retails sales of Ningxia wine in restaurants and wine shops in top cities like Beijing, Shanghai, Guangzhou, and others. In addition, Ningxia needs to continue to submit wines to both domestic and international wine competitions in order to gain feedback and, hopefully, more awards. They also want to develop a Ningxia International Wine Exchange and comprehensive Free Trade Zone.
- **Reinforcing the management of Ningxia Chateaux with Cru Classe Status.** As the strategic orientation of Ningxia wine industry is producing wine of high quality, the items listed in the regulations of the Ningxia Chateaux of Cru Classe system should be strictly followed. This includes stringent international evaluate of the vineyards, wines and chateaux of Cru Classe Status every two years.
- **Facilitation of wine tourism and culture.** Ningxia needs to continue to work on implementing their wine

tourism infrastructure with a focus on high quality wine, health, sport, and relaxation. In order to do this, they need to add additional elements of sightseeing, food, shopping, and entertainment into tourism offering. Additionally, they need to expand their base of vineyards, chateaux, restaurants, and sophisticated leisure activities, related to this theme.
- **Continued Development of Skills and New Jobs**. The Ningxia government recognizes it needs to continue to educate workers in viticulture, winemaking, wine tourism, marketing, and construction related to the wine industry.

Finally, Ningxia refuses to rest on its laurels and has expanded its vision for the future. The Comprehensive Planning of the Development of Wine Industry and Cultural Corridor believes that by the year 2020, vineyards in Ningxia will have increased to over 66,000 hectares. In addition to the establishment of a Grape Culture Center, they plan to build three ecological wine cities, ten wine-themed towns of different styles, and reach a level of at least 100 supreme chateaux. Their vision is to become the location of the greatest chateaux cluster in China, the biggest chateau wine-producing area in Asia, and one of the premier wine producing regions of the world.

## DISCUSSION QUESTIONS

1. Conduct a SWOT analysis on the Ningxia wine region, identifying Strengths, Weaknesses, Opportunities and Threats.
2. Analyze Ningxia's vision and strategy for the wine industry. How have they managed to achieve so much in such a short time? Will they be able to achieve their vision in the future?
3. What does Ningxia need to do to sustain its success? Identify

at least three success factors, and what they need to do to implement them.
4. Discuss the differences between wine tourism in China and other regions of the world, such as Bordeaux. What can the different regions learn from one another?
5. Assume you are in charge of wine tourism for Ningxia. What steps would you take to ensure a steady increase of tourists and revenue to the region in the next ten years, and achieve positive sustainability (respect for environment, equity of people, and economic return)?

www.ingramcontent.com/pod-product-compliance
Lightning Source LLC
Chambersburg PA
CBHW061223180526
45170CB00003B/1126